My Mom Jayne

A Daughter's Longing, Love, Loss and Legacy - From Bombshell to Broken Mirror

Jorge Hunter

Copyright Page

All rights reserved. No part of this publication may be reproduced, distributed, or transmitted in any form or by any means, including photocopying, recording, or other electronic or mechanical methods, without the prior written permission of the publisher, except in the case of brief quotations embodied in critical reviews and certain other noncommercial uses permitted by copyright law.

This book is an independent critical analysis and companion guide to the 2025 HBO documentary My Mom Jayne. All film titles, quotes, and trademarks referenced herein remain the property of their respective owners and are used under fair use for purposes of commentary, criticism, and scholarly review.

Copyright © 2025 by Jorge Hunter

Disclaimer

This book is a critical companion to the 2025 HBO documentary My Mom Jayne, offering commentary, interpretation, and expanded insight into the life of Jayne Mansfield as explored through the eyes of her daughter, Mariska Hargitay.

While every effort has been made to ensure factual accuracy and respectful representation, this guide is the work of an independent author (Jorge Hunte) and is not affiliated with, authorized by, or officially connected to HBO, Mariska Hargitay, or any individuals portrayed in the film. All trademarks, titles, and quotes belong to their respective owners and are used here under the principles of fair use for critical discussion and educational purposes.

This is not a retelling; it's a reexamination. The documentary is the catalyst; this book is the conversation that follows. Inside these pages, you'll find film analysis, emotional breakdowns, cultural context, and the hidden threads that connect a daughter's grief with a mother's misunderstood fame.

This guide is for the curious. The lovers of film. The seekers of truth. If you have ever wondered who Jayne Mansfield was beyond the bombshell; or who Mariska Hargitay became because of her, you've come to the right place.

Now, turn the page. The story isn't over; it's just beginning.

Table of Contents

Introduction
A Mirror to the Past

Chapter One - Who Was Jayne Mansfield?
Beneath the Blonde - The Real Vera Jayne Palmer
Crafted in Talent - The Creation of an Icon
The Mother and the Myth - A Dual Existence

Chapter Two - The Tragedy That Froze Time
The Night the World Went Silent
Three Small Survivors in the Backseat

Chapter Three - The Myth of Manufactured Stardom of Jayne Mansfield

The Studio Machine - Crafting a Blonde Bombshell

The Stereotype of The Dumb Blonde - The Brains Behind the Beauty

Publicity, Provocation, and the Price of Fame

Chapter Four - Mariska's Directorial Debut

Her Own Vision - The Making of My Mom Jayne

Cannes to HBO - A Triumph of Storytelling and Spirit

A Daughter's Closure, A Legacy Renewed

Chapter Five - Home Movies and Hidden Truths

Celluloid Memories - Revisiting Jayne's Private Tapes

Chapter Six - The Men in Her Life
The Husbands - Love, Lust, and Loss
The Affairs and the Allure

Chapter Seven - Scandal, Sex, and the 1960s Press
Tabloid Darling - How Jayne Played the Press
The Pink Palace and the Public Fantasy
From Bombshell to Punchline - The Fall from Favor

Chapter Eight - The Cannes Moment: When the World Watched Again
Mariska Walks the Croisette

The L'Œil d'or Nomination and What It Signified

Chapter Nine - A Legacy Rewritten
From Sex Symbol to Symbol of Strength

Conclusion
Stars Don't Die, They Transform

Introduction

A Mirror to the Past

Welcome to My Mom Jayne: A Daughter's Search, A Star Reclaimed. It begins with a photograph. A soft frame of platinum blonde hair, eyes that glimmer with unspoken dreams, and a smile that both invites and conceals. She was Jayne Mansfield; Hollywood's bodacious blonde, a woman sculpted by fame, desired by the masses, yet seldom understood. But for Mariska Hargitay, she was never just a sex symbol or a pop culture punchline. She was something infinitely more fragile, more sacred; the mother she barely knew.

In the 2025 HBO documentary My Mom Jayne, actress and advocate Mariska Hargitay takes on her most personal role yet; not in front of the camera, but behind it. As the director, she turns her lens on a life marked by fame and fatality, mystery and myth, longing and legacy. Premiering at the

Cannes Classics section of the 78th Cannes Film Festival, the film is no ordinary biographical tribute. It is a soulful excavation; a cinematic seance between a daughter and the mother time and tabloids had stolen away.

The film's resonance lies not just in the archival footage, the vintage glamour, or the Hollywood flashbacks, but in the aching vulnerability of its perspective. Through Mariska's eyes, viewers are invited to reimagine Jayne Mansfield not as the two-dimensional caricature history has offered, but as a layered, often lonely woman navigating the twin beasts of celebrity and motherhood.

This guidebook, My Mom Jayne: A Daughter's Search, A Star Reclaimed, is your passport into the deeper chambers of that journey. It isn't merely a retelling of events or a timeline of Mansfield's career. It's an exploration of grief, identity, and the curious legacy of living in someone's shadow while becoming a light of your own.

We begin with the facts we think we know. Jayne Mansfield: starlet, pinup, actress, headline-maker. Her tragic car accident in 1967 not only took her life but etched a cruel permanence to her image; the bombshell that died too young. Mariska was just three years old. Her memory of her mother isn't built from bedtime stories or home videos, but from fragments of cultural myth and whispers passed down like heirlooms. The documentary, and by extension this guide, seeks to collect those fragments, to piece together not just the life of a woman lost too soon, but the unfinished mother-daughter story that was halted by fate.

In My Mom Jayne, Mariska doesn't just want to tell her mother's story; she wants to understand it. The reels of footage, family conversations once too painful to have, and memories that flicker like old film, grainy but persistent. In doing so, she confronts her own silence, the decades she spent avoiding the full weight of her inheritance. The film is part confession, part catharsis. A reclamation of self and story.

It's no surprise then that when the film premiered at Cannes, it wasn't just the critics who leaned in; it was daughters, mothers, families, and fans who had also been touched by absence, haunted by stories left untold. For them, and for anyone who has longed to know the truth behind the face in the frame, this book is a companion, a deeper dive into the emotional, cultural, and cinematic threads woven through Mariska's film.

From the glitz of Hollywood premieres to the quiet grief behind closed doors, this guidebook follows every beat of the documentary and the personal truths it unveils. Whether you're here to rediscover a forgotten star or to witness the intimate unraveling of inherited sorrow, you're in for more than a film review. You're in for a resurrection.

So we begin not at the peak of Jayne Mansfield's fame, but at the crossroads of loss and curiosity. With a daughter's hand reaching back in time, not to grab headlines, but to hold the hand of the mother she never truly got to know. This is not nostalgia. This is reclamation.

Chapter One - Who Was Jayne Mansfield?

Beneath the Blonde - The Real Vera Jayne Palmer

Before she became the shimmering vision of 1950s glamour and tabloid fodder, Jayne Mansfield was simply Vera Jayne Palmer; an ambitious girl from Bryn Mawr, Pennsylvania, born in 1933, with a craving not just for attention, but for connection. Her father, Herbert Palmer, passed away when she was just three years old, a life-shaping loss that echoed eerily in her daughter Mariska's own origin story. Raised by her mother Vera Peers, young Jayne was academically gifted, emotionally perceptive, and relentlessly imaginative. Her early fascination with Shirley Temple gave way to grander aspirations; not merely to act, but to shine.

What many forget, or never knew, was how intelligent she was. Jayne could play the violin, spoke five languages, and had an IQ that hovered around 163. She wasn't content with being noticed; she wanted to command the room. And when she moved to Dallas and later Los Angeles, she realized that in the era of Monroe and Bardot, commanding attention often meant shaping herself into a particular image. So she did. But it was an image she both controlled and was confined by.

This chapter traces that metamorphosis; not as a fall from grace, but as a strategic rebranding by a woman who understood the value of performance. Interviews in the documentary reveal her diary entries, her handwritten letters, and moments of insecurity beneath the platinum facade. We see her not just as a bombshell, but as a tactician, a mother, a dreamer, and, paradoxically, a prisoner of her own creation.

Mariska Hargitay, narrating through archival letters and family memories, pieces together the fragments of her mother's authentic self; the version of Jayne that existed between photo ops and publicity stunts. The part we were not privileged to meet, because behind the glitz and glam, there were real moments.

Crafted in Talent - The Creation of an Icon

Hollywood in the 1950s was an illusionist's playground; a factory of fantasy where dreams were mass-produced and personalities custom-molded. Jayne Mansfield understood this system better than most. When she arrived in Tinseltown, she didn't wait to be discovered; she announced herself. With calculated pink outfits, impossibly dramatic entrances, and even staged wardrobe malfunctions, Jayne fed the machine that would one day consume her.

But she was no passive participant in her own fame. Archival interviews in the documentary reveal a woman deeply aware of her own commodification. Jayne once said; a forty-inch bust and a lot of perseverance will get you more than a cup of coffee, a lot more. It's a biting quote, usually read as satire, but in Hargitay's retelling, it becomes a bitter truth. Jayne was the master of her persona; until that persona became her master.

This subchapter spotlights studio deals, her infamous publicity stunts, and how she outmaneuvered the press to become one of the most photographed women in the world. I also explore her complicated rivalry with Marilyn Monroe; two blonde goddesses with radically different approaches to fame. Where Monroe was elusive, Mansfield was explosive. Where Marilyn whispered, Jayne roared. Yet both were victims of a culture that consumed women at their peak and discarded them just as quickly.

Film historians interviewed in the documentary offer fresh takes on Jayne's legacy; not as Monroe's shadow, but as a uniquely rebellious figure who weaponized her sexuality and broke molds, even as she seemed to play into them. Her movies, often dismissed as fluff, are reanalyzed here for their coded feminism and tragic undertones.

What emerges is the picture of a woman who walked a tightrope between fame and farce, liberation and exploitation. And at the heart of this balancing act was the irony; Jayne created the image that would eventually eclipse her soul.

The Mother and the Myth - A Dual Existence

In My Mom Jayne, Mariska Hargitay shares something that catches many off guard; the profound tenderness behind the flashbulbs. Despite the whirlwind of premieres, magazine covers, and scandalous headlines, Jayne Mansfield was a devoted mother of five. Home videos, narrated letters, and interviews with her surviving children paint a startling contrast to her public persona. At home, Jayne wasn't the seductress in a negligee; she was the mom baking cookies, braiding hair, singing lullabies.

This duality is at the emotional core of both the film and this chapter. How did Jayne juggle stardom and single motherhood in an era that offered no script for such a role? The answer is layered. Jayne brought her children into the spotlight; sometimes too eagerly, but she also fiercely protected them from its sharper edges. When she posed for Playboy, it was a business move. When she turned down roles, it was often because of her kids' schedules. She lived in a pink palace with heart-shaped bathtubs, but her refrigerator was stocked with school lunches.

The myth of Jayne Mansfield is impossible to escape, but within these pages, we offer a space where the myth and the mother coexist. Where the icon known for her curves and coyness is also remembered as a woman of courage, contradiction, and complexity. By the end of this chapter, readers are asked to confront their own assumptions about fame and femininity. What if the starlet wasn't a cautionary tale, but a case study in the high cost of visibility? What if, behind every wink and wardrobe stunt, there was a silent scream for recognition; not just as a body, but as a being?

Jayne Mansfield, it turns out, wasn't playing dumb. She was playing with us all. And beneath the blonde? A woman fighting not to disappear.

Chapter Two - The Tragedy That Froze Time

The Night the World Went Silent

It was June 29, 1967, when the glittering world of Hollywood was plunged into darkness. Jayne Mansfield, a woman whose name had become synonymous with glamour, allure, and tabloid fascination, was killed in a tragic car accident on a Louisiana highway. The moment the news broke, time stood still. Headlines screamed, Jayne Mansfield Dead at 34! and the world gasped in disbelief. The very embodiment of 1950s sensuality and charm had been silenced in a matter of seconds.

The documentary takes us into the heart of the tragedy, interweaving rare audio from emergency dispatch with haunting visuals of the aftermath. It is more than just the story of a crash; it is a moment that shifted cultural memory. Eyewitnesses speak of the sudden hush in the crowd gathered at the accident site, the surreal sight of the mangled Buick Electra, and the eerie quiet that followed the sirens.

Mariska Hargitay, just three years old at the time, was asleep in the backseat, shielded from physical harm by a combination of fate and seat placement. The documentary tenderly captures the emotional weight of that miracle; not only for Mariska, but for audiences reeling from the loss of a screen siren and the survival of a daughter. The imagery is symbolic; the flash of paparazzi bulbs now replaced with the harsh red and blue of police lights, a Hollywood fantasy shattered by the brutality of real life.

In this section, we also explore how media frenzy, sensational reporting, and conspiracy theories obscured the deeper tragedy; a mother lost, children orphaned, and a legacy thrown into question. Mansfield's death marked a chilling punctuation in the timeline of Hollywood's

Golden Age, closing the curtain on an era defined by its illusion of invincibility. My Mom Jayne does not just revisit the facts of the accident; it reframes them, layering emotion and perspective to transform what once was tabloid fodder into sacred narrative.

The press went into overdrive. Tabloids speculate wildly, some claiming Jayne had been decapitated, others questioning if it was truly an accident. The myth-making began instantly. The documentary challenges the narrative that consumed America's living rooms in 1967. Interviews with media historians and journalists offer a sobering critique of how female celebrities are reduced to headlines, even in death. One particularly poignant moment features Hargitay watching old news clippings; her face a portrait of disbelief and pain, as talking heads describe her mother's final moments with clinical detachment.

The film reframes this moment by emphasizing Mansfield's role as a mother. Family photos, tender letters, and home videos resurface to paint a fuller picture. These moments challenge the headlines, urging viewers to see beyond the tragic ending to the richness of Jayne's life. In doing so, it also mirrors Mariska's own journey, not just as a filmmaker but as a daughter rewriting her mother's legacy.

Letters of condolence, personal diary entries, and celebrity reactions are woven into the documentary to illustrate the cultural void she left behind. This section positions the tragedy not just as a personal loss but a collective mourning; a society grappling with the fragility of fame.

Three Small Survivors in the Backseat

Perhaps the most pacing revelation in My Mom Jayne is that three of Jayne's children were in the car during the crash; Mariska, Zoltan, and Miklós. Using deeply personal interviews with Hargitay and archival footage of her siblings, this section lays bare the long shadow of trauma. For Mariska, the accident wasn't just the end of a story; it was the beginning of a lifelong quest for identity and healing. Through her eyes, we see not only the tragedy but the resilience that followed.

The documentary powerfully blends past and present, showing Mariska as a child unaware of her mother's global fame and then as an adult confronting the emotional inheritance of that night. Viewers hear from family friends, child psychologists, and grief counselors who help contextualize the trauma of surviving such a public and violent loss. This isn't just about surviving a crash, it's about surviving a fractured narrative, one that the documentary tries to piece together with reverence.

Through photos left in a shoebox, voice recordings never before heard, and handwritten notes from Jayne to her children, the film crafts a mosaic of motherhood. Jayne, once dismissed as a blonde bombshell, is finally seen as the devoted mother she was.

It's a full-circle moment, both cinematic and spiritual. The three small survivors have grown, carrying with them the torch of a story finally being told right, not with scandal, but with soul. It is a resurrection, a reclamation, and most importantly, a daughter's love letter to the woman who gave her life, even as hers was cut short.

Chapter Three - The Myth of Manufactured Stardom of Jayne Mansfield

The Studio Machine - Crafting a Blonde Bombshell

Jayne Mansfield didn't just walk into Hollywood, she was built for it. Or, more accurately, she was built by it. In the 1950s and early '60s, the Hollywood studio system was an unstoppable force, creating icons, not discovering them. Much like a product launched to consumer frenzy, Jayne Mansfield was branded from the start. Her identity wasn't just molded; it was manufactured.

From her platinum-blonde hair to her hourglass figure and breathy voice, every detail of Jayne's public persona was designed to fit the mold of the blonde bombshell, a cultural archetype popularized by Marilyn Monroe. But while Monroe often seemed like the unwilling subject of projection, Mansfield embraced the spectacle. Or did she?

In her directorial debut, Mariska Hargitay explores how her mother's life was an exercise in performance. Jayne wasn't just playing a role onscreen; she was living it in every red carpet moment, every photo op, every appearance. Hollywood's formula for sex appeal involved symmetry and spectacle. Jayne was often given roles that required her to do little more than strut, giggle, and flirt. But this wasn't just typecasting, it was an economic model. Studio executives knew sex sold, and Jayne delivered like clockwork. Yet, as My Mom Jayne subtly reveals, beneath the layers of makeup and public relations polish was a woman who knew exactly what she was doing; and perhaps didn't always like it.

We explore Jayne's collaborations with Fox Studios, her role in The Girl Can't Help It, and the many magazine spreads that reinforced her star power. Through archival footage and expert commentary, Hargitay allows us to see the machinery behind the glamour. Mansfield was a product; but she was also a producer, a hustler, and a woman who, in many ways, tried to outsmart the very system that commodified her.

The Stereotype of The Dumb Blonde - The Brains Behind the Beauty

There's a dangerous lie often repeated in pop culture; beautiful women can't be smart. Jayne Mansfield was beautiful, undeniably so, but she was also brilliant. Holding a reported IQ of 163, she spoke five languages, played the violin, and had an academic background that shocked many who only knew her as a pin-up.

She understood the game Hollywood played and decided to play it better. Her strategic use of publicity; posing in skimpy outfits at precisely the right moment, showing up where she knew photographers would be, leveraging scandal to her advantage, it wasn't naivety. It was genius.

Mariska Hargitay's documentary offers rare glimpses into personal letters, interviews, and home footage that reveal a complex woman pushing against the cage she was handed. Jayne's comedic timing in films was often dismissed as mere caricature, but comedy is one of the hardest forms of performance; especially when layered with satire. In many ways, Jayne was satirizing the very roles she played.

We examine Jayne's appearances on talk shows, her clever deflections of sexist questions, and her off-screen wit. Journalists would often walk into an interview expecting a ditzy starlet and leave wondering if they'd just been intellectually outmaneuvered. Her laughter masked rebellion. Her curves distracted from her critique.

By presenting these facets of her personality, this segment of the documentary challenges viewers to question their own assumptions about women in entertainment. Did Jayne Mansfield play dumb, or was she playing us all?

Publicity, Provocation, and the Price of Fame

Jayne Mansfield was a master of the media long before Instagram influencers and TikTok celebrities existed. If there's one thing Mansfield understood better than anyone, it was the art of provocation. She knew how to command attention, and more importantly, how to convert it into headlines, and money.

From wardrobe malfunctions (many of which were likely intentional) to her infamous photo-bombing of Sophia Loren's cleavage-focused snapshot, Jayne understood how to manufacture buzz. Her life was a sequence of moments crafted for maximum exposure. But at what cost?

The Mariska Hargitay's film presents this dynamic through a deeply personal lens, exploring how the very tactics that catapulted Jayne into stardom also cornered her into an identity she could no longer escape.Her relationship with the press was symbiotic but volatile. Paparazzi were both her allies and her predators. She invited them in but could never close the door. The documentary details how even her tragedies were consumed as entertainment; none more glaring than her untimely death, which the tabloids devoured.

In interviews, friends and insiders recall Jayne's desire to be taken seriously, her dreams of doing Shakespeare, her longing to play dramatic roles, her frustrations with being locked into a single image. We see footage of Jayne attempting to break free from her blonde bombshell mold, often to resistance from studios and the public alike.

This final subchapter of Chapter Four paints a portrait of a woman who wielded her sexuality like a sword and a shield but was ultimately wounded by it. Through the lens of Hargitay's careful storytelling, the myth of Jayne Mansfield is deconstructed, and redefined. Fame wasn't just a spotlight; for Jayne, it became a trap.

Chapter Four - Mariska's Directorial Debut

Her Own Vision - The Making of My Mom Jayne

The journey from actress to director is never an easy one, especially for someone as publicly revered and privately reserved as Mariska Hargitay. Known to millions as the fierce and empathetic Olivia Benson from Law & Order: SVU, Hargitay's transition to filmmaking was marked by a deeply personal mission; to illuminate the life and legacy of her mother, Jayne Mansfield. The documentary My Mom Jayne is not just a project, it is a passion-fueled pilgrimage, a courageous reckoning with identity, loss, and maternal mystique.

Mariska was just three years old when her mother tragically died, and for years, her life was lived in the long shadow of a Hollywood legend she barely knew. This absence, though gaping, became a silent force in her life. The documentary became the vehicle through which she finally confronted her grief, curiosity, and longing. With the help of co-producer Trish Adlesic and cinematographer Tony Hardmon, the film evolved from a simple tribute into an artistic excavation of forgotten truths and buried wounds.

What makes the film unique is its layered perspective. Unlike conventional biographies, this story is told not by an outsider, but by a daughter searching for the woman behind the image. The interviews, archival footage, and private letters form a mosaic of Mansfield's life that we've never seen before, not as the bombshell but as the mother, the misfit, the dreamer, and the doomed star. Mariska's direction reveals not only Mansfield but also herself.

Technically, Mariska embraced a restrained but intimate approach. Avoiding the flashy overproduction that might have mirrored

Jayne's screen persona, she instead opted for a contemplative tone; dim lighting, soft piano scores by Max Avery Lichtenstein, and lingering close-ups. This style allowed emotions to surface organically. The interviews were not staged confrontations but healing conversations.

Most importantly, the documentary was filmed with emotional honesty. Hargitay didn't edit out her own tears, doubts, or revelations. The film feels like a therapy session turned cinematic experience. In doing so, she has crafted not just a documentary, but a generational healing process.

Cannes to HBO - A Triumph of Storytelling and Spirit

When My Mom Jayne premiered at the Cannes Classics section of the 78th Cannes Film Festival on May 17, 2025, it wasn't just another documentary debut. It was a cultural moment. The film received a standing ovation; not simply for its aesthetic or historical depth, but for the palpable heart that throbbed through every frame. The L'Œil d'or nomination was a prestigious nod, but the real reward was the emotional connection the film fostered with its audience.

Critics and fans alike noted that the documentary was far more than a celebrity profile. It was, in fact, a mother-daughter story that transcended the Hollywood trappings of fame and scandal. The world saw Jayne Mansfield; not just the pink-loving, publicity-craving icon, but a woman of contradictions; whip-smart, vulnerable, ambitious, and, ultimately, human.

The film's Cannes reception ignited international buzz. Reviewers from Variety and Vanity Fair praised Hargitay's courage and artistic poise. The media quickly turned its spotlight on the bombshell revelation Mariska shared during the press tour; a disclosure about her real biological father. This wasn't mere tabloid fodder. It reframed her personal narrative and emphasized the theme of reclaimed truth woven throughout the film.

From Cannes, the documentary will make its way to the Tribeca Festival on June 13, 2025, further affirming its place as a vital piece of cinematic storytelling. A limited theatrical release will follow on June 20 before its highly anticipated HBO premiere on June 27, ensuring that a broad and diverse audience would be able to experience the film.

The HBO release is a calculated and emotionally intelligent move. HBO, known for championing intimate, brave documentaries, provided the ideal platform. The broadcast set social media ablaze. Fans shared personal stories of mother loss, rediscovery, and emotional reconnection.

A Daughter's Closure, A Legacy Renewed

Mariska Hargitay's documentary is ultimately a story of closure; but not the tidy kind that erases pain. Rather, it offers an honest confrontation with the past and a renewal of the bond between mother and daughter, even in the absence of the living.

For Mariska, the filmmaking process was emotionally grueling. In press interviews, she admitted to questioning herself every step of the way. Am I doing her justice? Am I opening old wounds? Am I brave enough to face what I might find? These questions haunted her. But what she discovered along the way was not just a deeper understanding of Jayne Mansfield, but of herself. Through the documentary, she accepted that it was okay not to have all the answers. It was okay to love a myth and still mourn the woman.

The film renewed interest in Jayne Mansfield, not as a caricature but as a fully realized human being. Scholars began revisiting her roles, looking beyond the cleavage and into the craft. Feminist thinkers started analyzing Mansfield as a tragic figure of gendered exploitation and misunderstood genius. And most importantly, viewers across generations began to see her not as Marilyn Monroe's imitator, but as an icon in her own right.

Mariska's bravery opened a door. In making peace with her past, she encouraged others to do the same. Her vulnerability became a beacon for anyone grappling with inherited legacies, unanswered questions, or the silence left behind by loss.

The legacy of My Mom Jayne is twofold. It restored Jayne Mansfield's dignity and complexity. And it gave her daughter a voice, one strong enough to echo across decades. What began as a film became a movement, a meditation, and a monument.

As the credits roll, what stays with you isn't just the haunting image of a woman frozen in time, but the gentle rise of a daughter finally embracing her story. And in that embrace, we find a story that is both personal and profoundly universal.

Chapter Five - Home Movies and Hidden Truths

Celluloid Memories - Revisiting Jayne's Private Tapes

In a small wooden box tucked away for decades were reels of film that once captured the essence of Jayne Mansfield in her rawest, unfiltered state, moments not choreographed by studios, directors, or press agents. These private tapes, some dusty with age, some partially deteriorated, were unearthed by Mariska Hargitay and her team during the making of My Mom Jayne. The celluloid flickered to life with images of Jayne at home, laughing with her children, lounging by the pool, cooking in the kitchen, scenes that shattered the caricature of the blonde bombshell with a high-pitched giggle and instead revealed a present, loving, complex mother.

Mariska described these films as a visceral jolt to the soul, offering her a rare window into a mother she barely remembered. Seeing the technological process of film restoration showing faded images were revived, how audio was cleaned to recapture laughter, lullabies, and late-night conversations between Jayne and her children. Every frame became a puzzle piece, slowly reconstructing a woman who had been flattened by tabloids and headlines.

I also examine the impact these films had on the documentary's narrative arc. Instead of relying solely on third-party accounts, Mariska was able to narrate her mother's life through Jayne's own lens. The chapter highlights how these tapes reshaped the trajectory of the film and helped Mariska emotionally reconnect with her past. The celluloid memories became more than archival footage, they became a resurrection of memory, maternal warmth, and haunting absence.

Home videos often lie; not intentionally, but by omission. In front of the lens, even the most spontaneous moments are performative. Jayne Mansfield, known for her acute awareness of publicity, often used her camera as another means of self-production. In one clip, she preens playfully in a mirror, aware that she is being filmed. In another, she directs the children with a casual smile for the camera, creating memories that were not merely recorded but orchestrated. These moments raise profound questions about authenticity. Was Jayne performing even in her most private moments? And if so, what was she trying to protect or preserve?

A scene of Jayne singing softly to baby Mariska could be read as maternal tenderness or a strategic portrayal of domesticity. The ambiguity of these moments became a critical feature of My Mom Jayne. Viewers are invited to form their own interpretations: Was this the real

Jayne Mansfield, or was she always acting, even when the curtains were drawn?

Additionally, this guide examines the editing choices; what footage was used, what was excluded, and why. Was it fair to dissect and display these private moments decades after her death? To tell the story of Jayne Mansfield meant more than just examining film footage; it required digging through layers of family archives, personal artifacts, letters, and mementos that had long been buried both literally and emotionally.

Old Valentine's Day cards, drawings made by her children, Jayne's perfume bottles, wardrobe sketches, and a lock of baby Mariska's hair were among the hundreds of items cataloged for this project. But more than curatorial efforts, these moments became portals into a life interrupted; each item breathing life into a fading memory.

Mariska's emotional journey is front and center here. The documentary, as this subchapter explores, was not just a film project but a pilgrimage of healing. In her own words, she compared the process to unboxing my grief, one object at a time. The chapter also examines how other family members contributed to this emotional excavation, often sharing insights or revealing stories that had remained untold for decades.

There's also a broader conversation about legacy; how do we preserve memory without distorting it? What stories do we choose to pass down, and what truths are we too afraid to confront? My Mom Jayne becomes a microcosm of this larger human experience, the effort to find oneself through the fragments left behind by those we've loved and lost. In combing through the ashes, Mariska finds not just Jayne, but herself. This chapter underscores how home movies and hidden truths shape not only the legacy of Jayne Mansfield but also the emotional architecture of her daughter's identity.

Chapter Six - The Men in Her Life

The Husbands - Love, Lust, and Loss

Jayne Mansfield's love life was as sensational as her career. Her marriages were more than just romantic escapades; they were performances themselves, complete with dazzling entrances, dramatic plot twists, and bittersweet finales. Jayne's three marriages, beginning with Paul Mansfield, the man whose last name she would famously keep. Their early love was raw and rooted in youthful ambition, but it quickly gave way to the pressures of fame and motherhood.

Her second husband, Mickey Hargitay, a former Mr. Universe, seemed tailor-made for Hollywood's fantasy couple narrative. Together, they were a spectacle; statuesque, photogenic, and unapologetically theatrical. But behind the curtain, tensions simmered.

Mickey admired Jayne's charisma, but struggled with the ways it eclipsed his own career. Their relationship, while passionate, was fraught with jealousy and competition.

Her final husband, Matt Cimber, was the most enigmatic of the three. A theater director, he tried to steer Jayne into more serious acting, but their visions clashed. Their short-lived marriage was marked by creative friction and personal disillusionment. As Jayne sought validation beyond her sex symbol image, Matt's attempts to reshape her career only widened the emotional chasm between them.

In the documentary, Mariska Hargitay revisits these marriages not through gossip, but through the lens of a daughter seeking understanding. Through letters, home footage, and surviving interview reels, she peels back the tabloid varnish and exposes the emotional truths each marriage carried. These relationships weren't just romantic entanglements; they were turning points that shaped Jayne's evolution as a woman and performer.

The Affairs and the Allure

Jayne Mansfield's love life didn't stop at her husbands. Her allure extended into notorious affairs that blurred the lines between lust, ambition, and genuine affection. From rumored romances with John F. Kennedy to flirtations with powerful producers, Jayne's private life was fodder for the tabloids; but the truth, as this subchapter reveals, was far more complex.

She was a woman who understood her effect on men. In an era that demanded women be demure and dependent, Jayne wielded her sexuality as power. But that power came at a cost. Many of the men drawn to her were intoxicated by her image rather than her intellect or heart. We gain insight into how Jayne navigated these entanglements; with agency, calculation, and at times, heartbreak.

In a society quick to vilify female sexuality, Jayne's affairs became tools for public shaming. Yet, the documentary doesn't exploit her; instead, it reclaims her narrative. Mariska Hargitay confronts these stories not to sensationalize them, but to understand the emotional truth within them. Was Jayne searching for love or validation? Was she playing a role, or simply trying to survive a world that only valued her body?

This subchapter confronts the blurred lines between empowerment and objectification, capturing Jayne's magnetic pull and the emotional consequences of living inside a myth she helped build; but couldn't always control.

Perhaps the most poignant revelation of My Mom Jayne is Mariska Hargitay's discovery about her biological father; a secret long buried beneath layers of family lore and media distortion. Jayne's first husband, Paul Mansfield, was long believed to be Mariska's biological father. However, as revealed in the documentary, Jayne carried a private truth; Mariska's biological father was someone else, a man whose identity had been protected, even denied, for decades. Through archival materials, family interviews, and candid monologues, Mariska lifts the veil on this personal truth.

What emerges is a story of identity and emotional reckoning and what it meant for a young girl growing up in the shadow of her mother's fame. It's a journey of connection, of loss, and ultimately of healing. Jayne Mansfield's relationship with the father of Mariska is shown to be complicated, one marked by secrecy, desire, and emotional stakes that went far beyond public appearances. The documentary's brave decision to spotlight this revelation speaks volumes about Mariska's courage and the depth of her search for truth.

In unpacking this hidden chapter, the film reframes Jayne not only as a public figure, but as a mother who protected her daughter with both ferocity and fragility. This subchapter is a raw, emotional arc that ties together the themes of identity, secrecy, and maternal love that pulse throughout the documentary.

Together, these subchapters offer a powerful and emotionally complex portrait of Jayne Mansfield's relationships; not as tabloid spectacle, but as deeply human experiences that left lasting imprints on her life and the life of her daughter.

Chapter Seven - Scandal, Sex, and the 1960s Press

Tabloid Darling - How Jayne Played the Press

In the whirlwind of post-war Hollywood glitz, Jayne Mansfield reigned as the quintessential media muse. With every calculated wink, wardrobe malfunction, and baby-doll giggle, Jayne crafted a persona not just to be admired; but to be consumed. In this chapter, we explore how Jayne Mansfield masterfully manipulated the press, understanding instinctively that publicity was currency and scandal its golden coin.

Drawing from Mariska Hargitay's documentary insights, this subchapter unveils how Jayne didn't merely fall victim to media sensationalism; she leaned into it. From her orchestrated appearances at pool parties where accidents conveniently happened, to her headline-grabbing quotes; like claiming her IQ was higher than Einstein's. Jayne knew how to be in control of her own image. The documentary reveals rare archival footage and press clippings that show how Jayne's publicist-driven stunts turned her into a household name.

But was Jayne in control, or was she ultimately a prisoner of her own brand?

The Pink Palace and the Public Fantasy

Jayne Mansfield's famed home; The Pink Palace, wasn't just a residence. It was a mythic space that blurred the lines between reality and fantasy. Decorated with floor-to-ceiling heart-shaped bathtubs, pink shag carpets, and cupids galore, the mansion was Jayne's glittering tribute to her public persona. It was the stage where her life and performance became indistinguishable.

For the public, it was a dream factory; for Jayne, it was part sanctuary, part trap. The mansion became an emblem of 1950s and 60s consumerist excess and gendered expectations. With commentary from architectural historians and Hollywood insiders, we explore how Jayne used her home as a narrative device, staging photoshoots and press events in her own domestic fairy tale.

Mariska's direction ensures that the Pink Palace is not just a backdrop but a character in Jayne's story. Through its rose-colored walls and heart-shaped furnishings, we see Jayne's hunger to control her myth, but also the ache of a woman who was always performing, even at home.

From Bombshell to Punchline - The Fall from Favor

As the 1960s marched toward counterculture revolution, Jayne

Mansfield's brand of overt sexuality and tongue-in-cheek glamour began to lose its shimmer. Once celebrated for her risqué antics, she found herself mocked and diminished by a press that had once crowned her queen. The media that helped her rise began to tear her down, portraying her not as an icon, but as a caricature.

The documentary unpacks these moments with chilling clarity; showing how the same tools Jayne once wielded began to betray her. Interviews with cultural critics and contemporaries reveal how misogyny and shifting societal norms played a role in the public's waning fascination.

The chapter also touches on Jayne's increasing exclusion from prestigious Hollywood projects, how she navigated roles in B-movies and European films, and her desperate attempts to remain relevant. Through Mariska's emotional narration, the viewers; and the readers, come to understand the loneliness behind the glitter.

Jayne Mansfield, once a symbol of sexual freedom, became a punchline in a cruel media circus she helped build.

Ultimately, this chapter is not just about Jayne. It's about fame, media ethics, and the price of reinvention in a world that builds women up only to delight in their undoing.

Chapter Eight - The Cannes Moment: When the World Watched Again

Mariska Walks the Croisette

Cannes. A name that evokes cinematic prestige, history, and global spotlight. On May 17, 2025, the Croisette played host to a deeply personal unveiling; the premiere of My Mom Jayne in the Cannes Classics section.

For Mariska Hargitay, it was not just a film festival appearance; it was a symbolic return of her mother to the screen, decades after her untimely death. Dressed in elegance, flanked by her family, and surrounded by global press, Mariska's journey to Cannes is painted not as a publicity stunt but as a sacred pilgrimage to restore and honor her mother's cinematic legacy. We see Mariska's reflections as revealed in press interviews and her trembling speech at the post-screening Q&A.

The emotional resonance of the documentary was palpable; audiences wept, critics stood in ovation, and the ghosts of Hollywood's golden era seemed to flicker alive on the screen. Through compelling prose and narrative flair, we explore how the festival became the perfect backdrop for this intergenerational reclamation of identity.

The standing ovation at Cannes was only the beginning. My Mom Jayne sparked critical discourse across continents. The praise that highlighted the intimate storytelling, raw archival footage, and the feminist reclamation of a woman too long reduced to her curves and scandals. Yet, beyond reviews, I examine the ripple effect among viewers.

Social media exploded with hashtags, tributes, and personal stories from fans who felt seen, heard, or inspired by Jayne and

Mariska's intertwined stories. Film scholars began to reevaluate Mansfield's position in cinematic history. Was she truly just a blonde bombshell? Or had we, as a society, overlooked the brains beneath the beauty?

It became a cultural reckoning. Jayne Mansfield, once dismissed as a caricature of 1950s Hollywood excess, was now being repositioned as a layered, tragic, and fiercely intelligent woman whose life was worth scholarly consideration and empathetic remembrance.

The L'Œil d'or Nomination and What It Signified

Perhaps the most telling validation came in the form of a nomination for the prestigious L'Œil d'or award, given to the best documentary at Cannes. Exploring what this recognition meant; not just for Mariska, but for female directors, legacy films, and children of iconic figures trying to reclaim familial truth.

I detail the competitive field of documentaries this year and position My Mom Jayne within the narrative of documentaries that blend personal discovery with cultural significance. Through interviews with jury members, snippets from acceptance speeches, and reflective essays, I capture the undercurrent of pride and awe that accompanied the nomination.

But this isn't just about accolades. It's about symbolic justice. The L'Œil d'or nomination validated Jayne Mansfield's story as worthy of intellectual and artistic consideration, not just tabloid fascination.

Mariska's lens; both figuratively and literally, transformed tragedy into triumph. Each section of this chapter blends emotion, cultural analysis, and cinematic critique to paint a vivid picture of Jayne Mansfield's posthumous revival and the daughter who made the world pause to watch again.

Chapter Nine - A Legacy Rewritten

From Sex Symbol to Symbol of Strength

Jayne Mansfield was long entombed in the golden coffin of Hollywood's one-dimensional portrayals; a bombshell, a blonde, a scandal. But in My Mom Jayne, Mariska Hargitay artfully wields the camera like a sculptor's chisel, carving away myth to reveal muscle. The nuanced reframing of Jayne's identity; from a pin-up paragon of the 1950s and 1960s to a complex woman who weaponized her image in a male-dominated world. Interviews from feminist scholars, illustrated with rare behind-the-scenes clips and deeply personal family footage, paint Jayne as a trailblazer rather than a victim of her own caricature. What emerges is a new symbol; not of lust, but of layered femininity, resilience, and reclamation. This reframing not only changes how we view Jayne, but challenges how we define womanhood across eras.

It is about absence, longing, and the alchemy of grief. I trace Mariska's evolution from orphaned daughter to cinematic storyteller. Drawing from diary entries, retrieved voice notes, and candid interviews, the narrative captures the filmmaker's intimate search for meaning through art. The documentary, therefore, is not just a tribute; it's a metamorphosis; a reclamation of voice from silence, of presence from absence. The reader is invited to journey with Mariska as she transforms trauma into testimony, producing not only a film, but a personal rebirth.

Legacy, like memory, is mutable. It bends with every retelling, every revelation, every archival unboxing. Her once-sensationalized image is now being analyzed through the lens of gender politics, body autonomy, and celebrity culture. The documentary becomes more than a film; it becomes a catalyst for re-remembering; poignant reminder that stories evolve, and so too can icons.

Jayne Mansfield may have been forgotten by history's mainstream, but through her daughter's lens, she becomes unforgettable in all the right ways.

Conclusion

Stars Don't Die, They Transform

Jayne Mansfield, even in death, transcended the fragile confines of mortality. The final chapter of her life was not written in the crash that claimed her body, but in the echo of her legacy; loud, unapologetic, and mythically enduring. Through Mariska Hargitay's lens, the narrative of Jayne's life breaks free from the exploitation that plagued her public image, restoring dimension to a figure once flattened by media sensationalism. Mansfield's legacy evolves into an anthem for every woman dismissed for her beauty and underestimated for her intellect. Her transformation from tabloid tragedy to cultural touchstone is one of the documentary's most profound triumphs.

As much as this documentary is about Jayne Mansfield, it is equally a testament to

Mariska Hargitay's journey of reclamation and healing. The camera allowed Mariska to process long-buried grief, uncover truths, and reintroduce herself to the mother she barely knew. The documentary becomes a diary, a mirror, and a voice recorder; capturing fragments of memory and emotion and piecing them together into a cohesive, healing whole.

Jayne Mansfield's story is emblematic of a larger Hollywood narrative; the way the industry crafts, consumes, and discards its women. Through Jayne's life and Mariska's storytelling, we revisit an era of impossible standards and toxic tabloid culture. But more importantly, we witness a reckoning; one that calls for more humane narratives, richer portrayals, and industry accountability. Jayne's story, recontextualized through a modern lens, becomes not just historical reflection but cultural critique.

This final chapter examines how My Mom Jayne will live on beyond its HBO release and film festival acclaim. It's not just a film; it's a conversation starter, a tool for healing, and an invitation for viewers to reimagine the stories of their own pasts. Mansfield's name, once synonymous with scandal and skin, now carries the weight of survival, maternal strength, and artistic agency. I conclude by reflecting on the film's emotional impact on audiences, its potential to inspire future biographical storytelling, and the unshakable truth that stars like Jayne Mansfield never truly die; they simply transform into something more luminous.

Printed in Dunstable, United Kingdom